CH

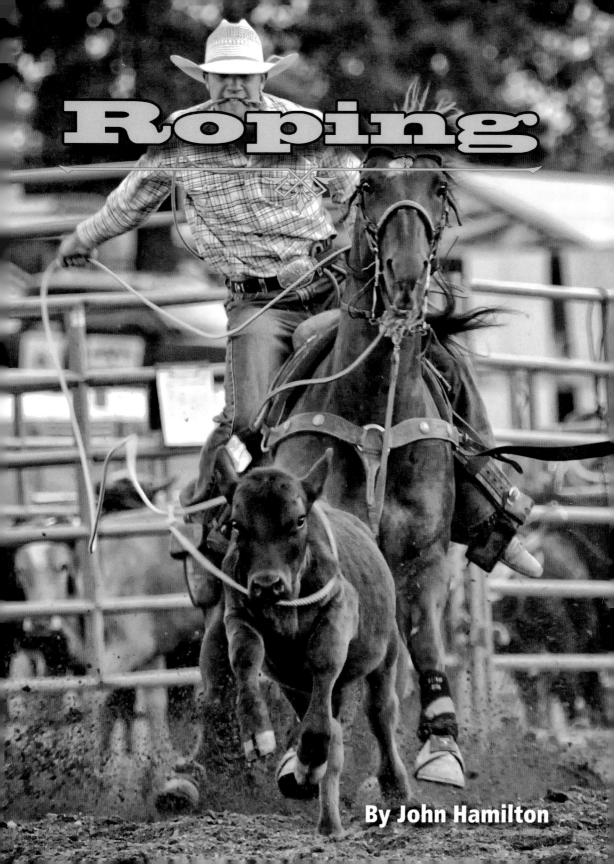

Roping

By John Hamilton

Visit us at
www.abdopublishing.com

Published by ABDO Publishing Company, PO Box 398166, Minneapolis, MN 55439. Copyright ©2014 by Abdo Consulting Group, Inc. International copyrights reserved in all countries. No part of this book may be reproduced in any form without written permission from the publisher. A&D Xtreme™ is a trademark and logo of ABDO Publishing Company.

Printed in the United States of America, North Mankato, Minnesota.
052013
092013

Editor: Sue Hamilton
Graphic Design: John Hamilton
Cover: John Hamilton
Photos: All photos by John Hamilton, except: ThinkStock-pg 5;
Tom Baker, pg 30-31.

ABDO Booklinks
Web sites about rodeos are featured on our Book Links pages. These links are routinely monitored and updated to provide the most current information available. Web site: www.abdopublishing.com

Library of Congress Control Number: 2013931684

Cataloging-in-Publication Data

Hamilton, John.
 Roping / John Hamilton.
   p. cm. -- (Xtreme rodeo)
ISBN 978-1-61783-982-5
1. Calf roping--United States--Juvenile literature. 2. Steer roping--United
   States--Juvenile literature. 3. Team roping--United States--Juvenile
   literature.   I. Title.
791.8/4--dc23
                              2013931684

Contents

Roping History

Rodeo roping events have their roots in ranching. On the plains of the Old West, roping was a chore that ranchers had to perform every day. Even today, cowboys rope cattle and other livestock to be rounded up for branding or medical care. Roping is a skill that takes a lot of practice. It is also a thrilling crowd pleaser that's always fun to watch.

Tie-Down Roping

Tie-down roping is the most complicated event in rodeo competition. It combines roping skills, horsemanship, and athletic ability. Cowboys compete against the clock to see who can rope and tie a calf in the shortest time.

"Rodeo" is a Spanish word used by early cowboys when they gathered up their cattle. The English translation is "round up."

Tie-down roping begins with the cowboy on horseback waiting in a fenced area called the "box." A breakaway rope barrier is placed in front of the box. A calf waits in a pen called a "chute." When the cowboy nods his head, spring-loaded doors on the chute open and the calf bursts into the arena. The calf is always given a head start. When the rope barrier on the box drops, the cowboy and his horse chase the calf.

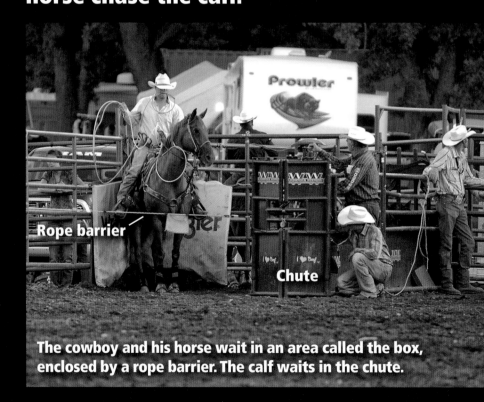

Rope barrier

Chute

The cowboy and his horse wait in an area called the box, enclosed by a rope barrier. The calf waits in the chute.

Spring-loaded doors on the chute open, and the calf exits. When it runs a set distance, the rope barrier drops.

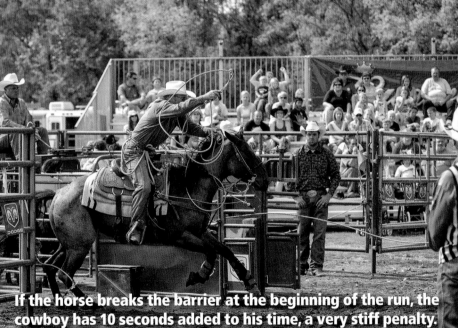

If the horse breaks the barrier at the beginning of the run, the cowboy has 10 seconds added to his time, a very stiff penalty.

The cowboy throws his rope from horseback, then leaps to the ground and runs to the calf. Simultaneously, the cowboy's well-trained horse backs up to take up the slack in the rope.

The cowboy grabs the calf and throws it to the ground on its side. He then ties the calf with a six-foot (1.8-m) rope called a piggin' string. He ties three legs together using a half-hitch knot, called a "hooey." Then the roper throws his hands in the air to signal he's finished, and the timer stops.

As the cowboy wrestles the calf to the ground, he keeps the piggin' string clenched in his teeth until needed.

The cowboy ties three legs together using a half-hitch knot, called a "hooey."

When the cowboy is finished, he throws his hands in the air and the timer stops.

After the calf is tied up, the cowboy remounts his horse and lets up the slack on the rope. The calf must remain tied for six seconds. If it frees itself, the cowboy receives no score. In tie-down roping, nine seconds is considered a good time. Top rodeo competitors score about seven or eight seconds.

Calves must be weaned from their mothers and weigh between 220 and 280 pounds (100-127 kg). The animals are very rarely injured.

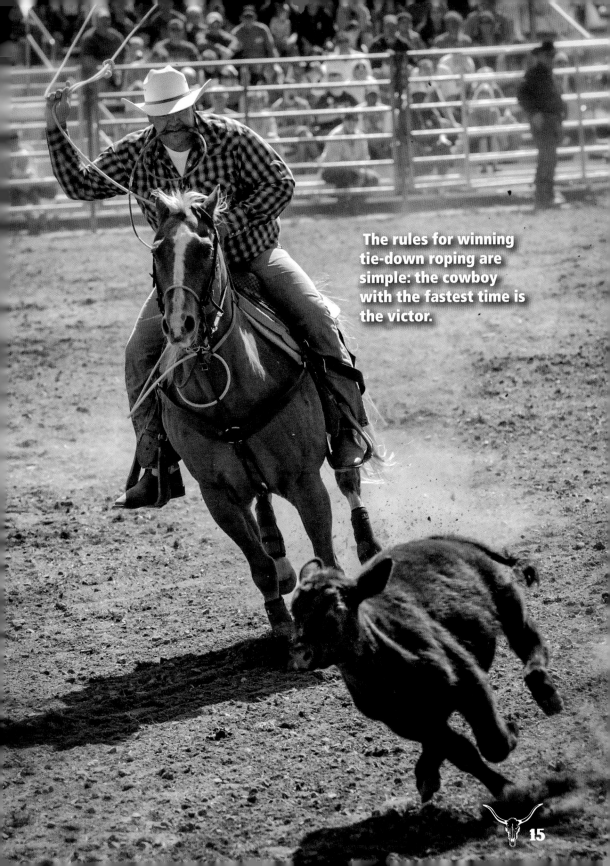

The rules for winning tie-down roping are simple: the cowboy with the fastest time is the victor.

A well-trained horse is extremely important in tie-down roping. It must be fast and nimble. It must follow directions. It also must move as the calf moves, dodging and weaving around the arena. A champion tie-down roping horse can cost well over $100,000.

Breakaway Roping

Breakaway roping is similar to tie-down roping. Once the competitor ropes the calf, the horse comes to a halt. The other end of the rope is tied to the saddle horn by a thin string. The rope is pulled tight and the string, with an easy-to-see flag attached, breaks away. The timer then stops, and the quickest time wins. Breakaway roping is most often seen in junior rodeos, high school rodeos, and college rodeos.

Breakaway rope and flag

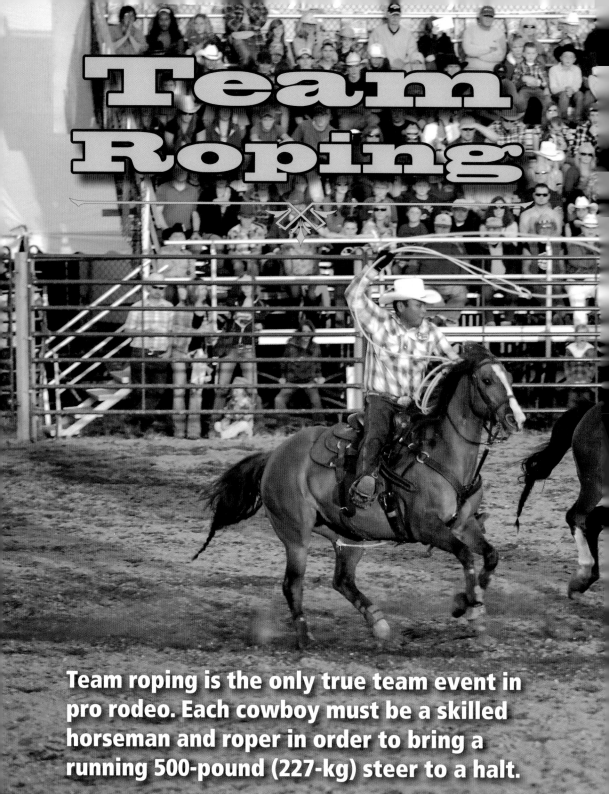

Team Roping

Team roping is the only true team event in pro rodeo. Each cowboy must be a skilled horseman and roper in order to bring a running 500-pound (227-kg) steer to a halt.

Team roping closely mirrors
skills used on ranches today.

Team roping begins much like tie-down roping. Two cowboys on horseback wait in fenced off "boxes" on either side of a narrow chute. When a steer is released from the chute, it's given a head start. Then the horsemen start the chase, with the hope of roping the steer in the fastest time.

Like tie-down roping, if a horse breaks the barrier at the beginning of the run, the team has 10 seconds added to its time.

The first cowboy to rope the steer is called the "header." He ropes the steer by the horns or neck. There are three legal catches. They include roping the neck, both horns, or the head and one horn.

Steers are protected from injury by leather horn wraps.

After the header has done his work, the second cowboy, the "heeler," attempts to rope the steer's hind feet. The timer stops when both cowboys' horses are turned to face each other. Winning times often range from four to six seconds.

Modern rodeo rope is made of synthetic fibers, with a smooth finish. It is stiff and holds its shape when thrown.

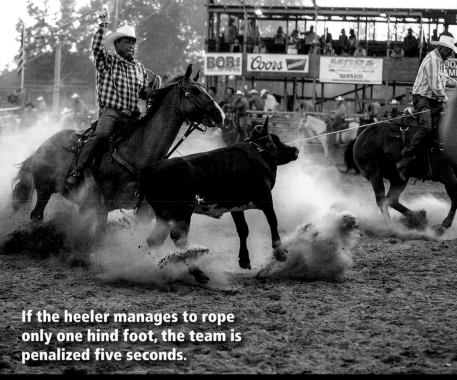

If the heeler manages to rope only one hind foot, the team is penalized five seconds.

Well-trained horses are very important in team roping. American quarter horses are often used. They have good "cow sense" and can anticipate a steer's movements. Their training is specialized, depending on if they are ridden by headers or heelers.

Steers in team roping competition are usually Corriente cattle that weigh about 500 pounds (227 kg). They are even-tempered and sturdy enough for roping.

The Professional Rodeo Cowboys Association (PRCA) has strict rules to make sure rodeo livestock are treated humanely. Veterinarians are always on hand at PRCA-sanctioned rodeos to care for the animals.

Glossary

Corriente Steer

Most rodeo steers are Corriente steers. They are somewhat small, athletic, with upcurving horns, and have good endurance.

Hooey

The name given to the half-hitch knot used to tie a calf's legs together in tie-down roping competition.

Piggin' String

A six-foot (1.8-m) rope used to tie the feet of a calf in tie-down roping competition.

Professional Rodeo Cowboys Association

The world's largest and oldest rodeo sanctioning organization. It ensures that rodeos meet high standards in working conditions and livestock welfare. Located in Colorado Springs, Colorado, it sanctions about 600 rodeos in the U.S. and Canada.

Timed Event

A rodeo event, such as tie-down roping and team roping, in which contestants compete against the clock and themselves. The other kind of rodeo contest is the rough stock event, such as bull riding, which pits human versus animal.

Index

Champion team ropers Garrison Dixon (left) and Mel Potter (right).